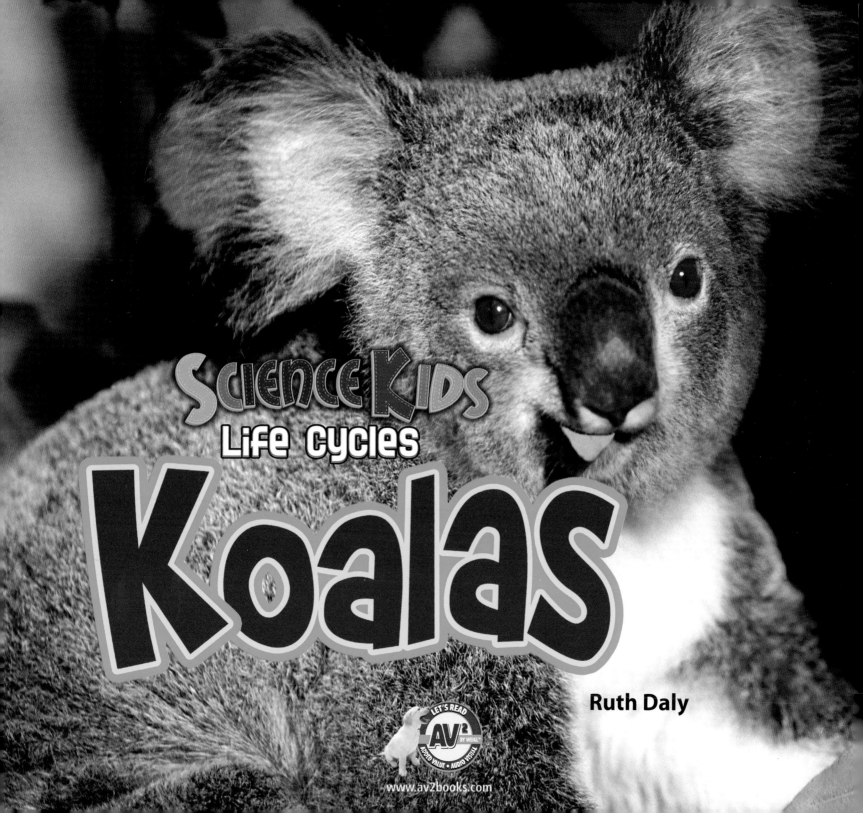

SCIENCE KIDS
Life cycles
Koalas

Ruth Daly

www.av2books.com

LET'S READ
AV²
BY WEIGL™
ADDED VALUE • AUDIO VISUAL

Go to **www.av2books.com**, and enter this book's unique code.

BOOK CODE

V939235

AV² by Weigl brings you media enhanced books that support active learning.

AV² provides enriched content that supplements and complements this book. Weigl's AV² books strive to create inspired learning and engage young minds in a total learning experience.

Your AV² Media Enhanced books come alive with...

Audio
Listen to sections of the book read aloud.

Video
Watch informative video clips.

Embedded Weblinks
Gain additional information for research.

Try This!
Complete activities and hands-on experiments.

Key Words
Study vocabulary, and complete a matching word activity.

Quizzes
Test your knowledge.

Slide Show
View images and captions, and prepare a presentation.

... and much, much more!

Published by AV² by Weigl
350 5ᵗʰ Avenue, 59ᵗʰ Floor New York, NY 10118
Websites: www.av2books.com   www.weigl.com

Library of Congress Control Number: 2014941059

ISBN 978-1-4896-1330-1 (hardcover)
ISBN 978-1-4896-1331-8 (softcover)
ISBN 978-1-4896-1332-5 (single user eBook)
ISBN 978-1-4896-1333-2 (multi-user eBook)

Printed in the United States of America in North Mankato, Minnesota
1 2 3 4 5 6 7 8 9 0 18 17 16 15 14

052014
WEP220514

Project Coordinator: Jared Siemens
Art Director: Terry Paulhus

Weigl acknowledges Getty Images as the primary image supplier for this title.

SCIENCE KIDS
Life Cycles
Koalas

CONTENTS

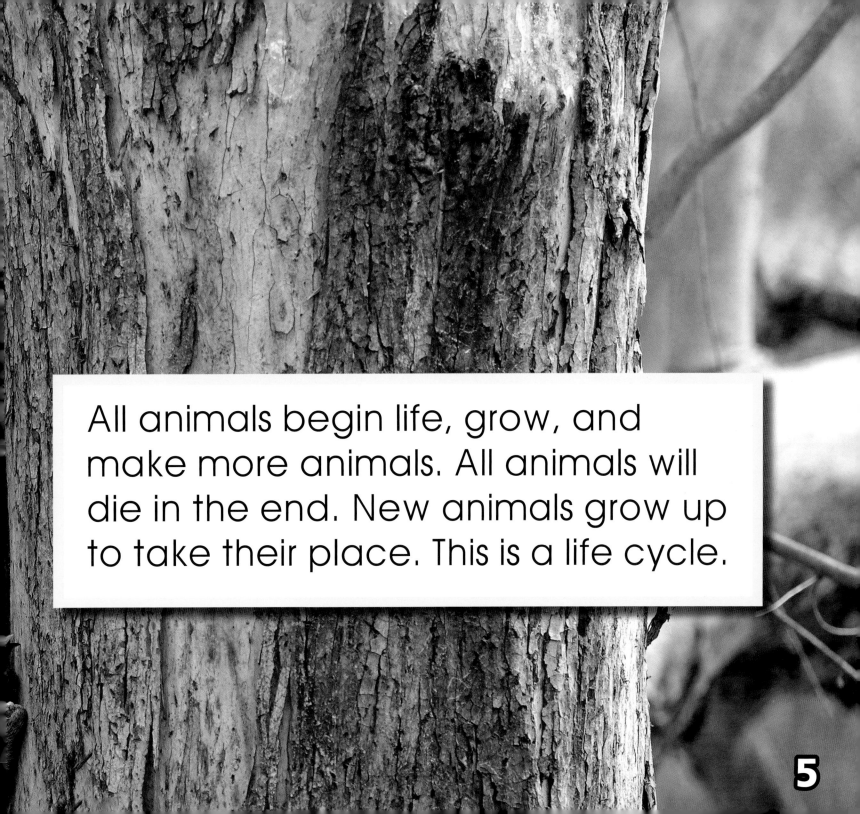

All animals begin life, grow, and make more animals. All animals will die in the end. New animals grow up to take their place. This is a life cycle.

6

Koalas live in Australia. They are marsupials. Marsupials have a pouch on the front of their bodies. This pouch is like a pocket.

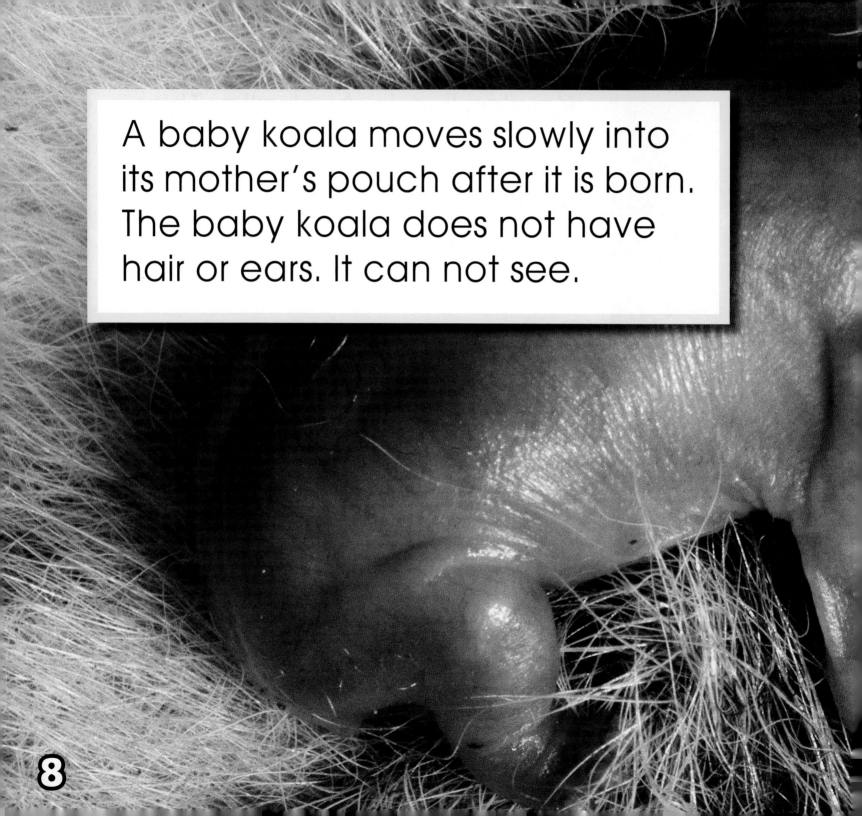

A baby koala moves slowly into its mother's pouch after it is born. The baby koala does not have hair or ears. It can not see.

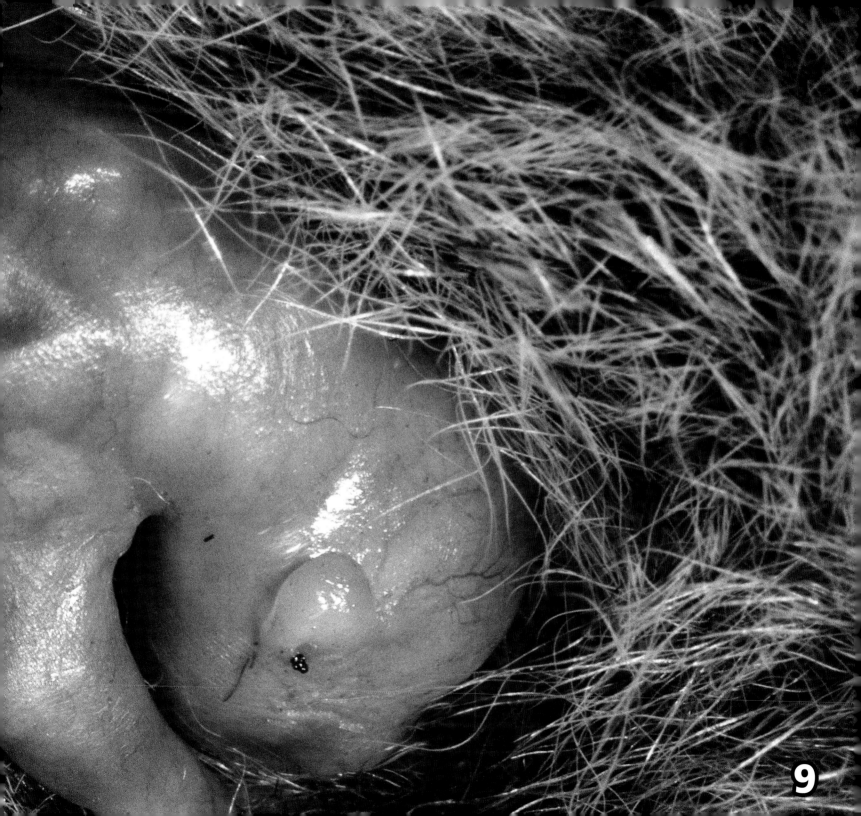

10

A baby koala is called a joey. The joey lives in its mother's pouch. It drinks milk from its mother. This milk helps the joey grow. The joey soon opens its eyes. It also starts to grow soft gray fur.

The mother feeds the joey
a soft food called pap.
Pap helps the joey grow.
Koalas have strong arms
to help them climb trees.

The joey may grow too big for the pouch. The mother then carries it on her back.

Joeys keep close to their mothers. The mother will keep the joey safe.

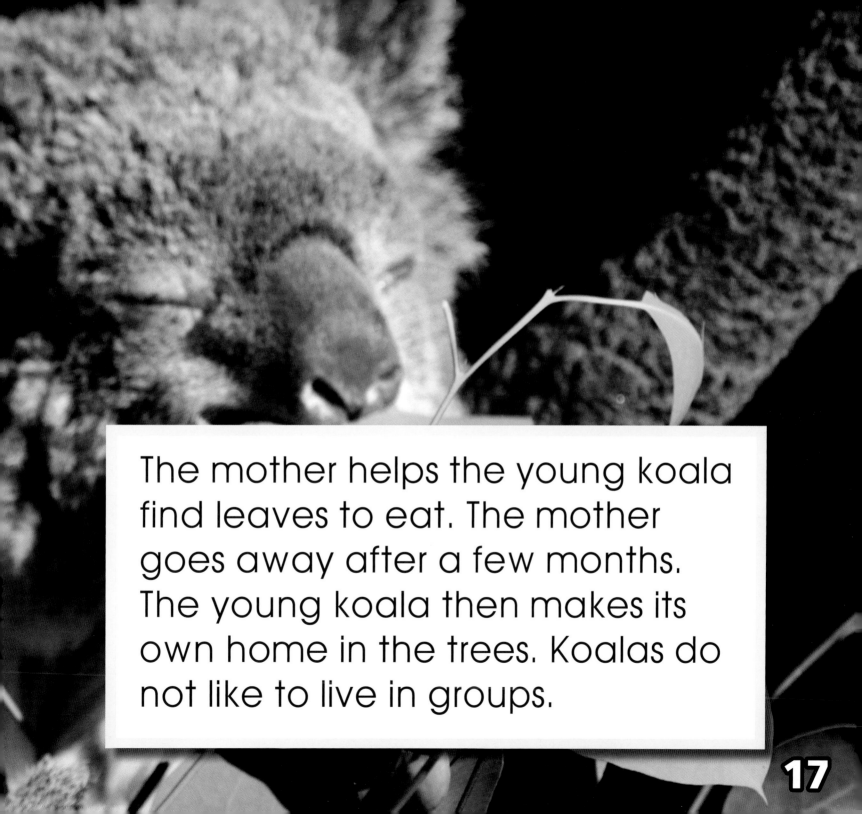

The mother helps the young koala find leaves to eat. The mother goes away after a few months. The young koala then makes its own home in the trees. Koalas do not like to live in groups.

Male and female koalas can be parents in the adult stage of the life cycle. The baby koala grows in its mother for about 35 days. Koalas can only have one baby at a time.

Koalas can be different sizes and colors. Joeys will be the same size and color as their parents.

Life Cycles Quiz

Test your knowledge of koala life cycles by taking this quiz. Look at these pictures. Which stage of the life cycle do you see in each picture?

adult   joey
baby   parent

22

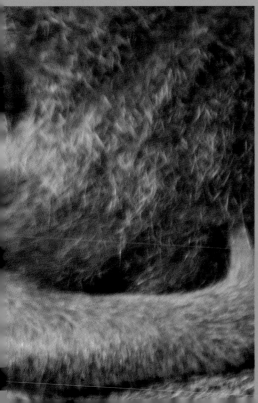

KEY WORDS

Research has shown that as much as 65 percent of all written material published in English is made up of 300 words. These 300 words cannot be taught using pictures or learned by sounding them out. They must be recognized by sight. This book contains 79 common sight words to help young readers improve their reading fluency and comprehension. This book also teaches young readers several important content words, such as proper nouns. These words are paired with pictures to aid in learning and improve understanding.

Page	Sight Words First Appearance
5	a, all, and, animals, end, grow, in, is, life, make, more, place, new, take, the, their, this, to, up, will
7	are, have, like, live, of, on, they
8	after, can, does, into, it, its, mother, not, see
11	also, eyes, from, helps, opens, soon
12	food, them, trees
15	back, big, close, for, her, keep, may, then, too
17	after, away, do, eat, few, find, groups, home, leaves, makes, months, own, young
18	about, at, be, days, one, only, time
20	as, be, different, same, when

Page	Content Words First Appearance
5	life cycle
7	Australia, bodies, koalas, marsupials, pocket, pouch
8	baby, ears, hair
11	fur, joey, milk
12	arms, pap
19	adult, parents, stage
20	colors, sizes

Check out www.av2books.com for activities, videos, audio clips, and more!

1 Go to www.av2books.com.

2 Enter book code. **V 9 3 9 2 3 5**

3 Fuel your imagination online!

www.av2books.com